Presented to:

_____

By:

_____

Date:

_____

DEDICATION

To Cindy Secrest McDowell:
Lover of quilts
and a "patchwork" mom

J.Z.

Faith Kids® is an imprint of
Cook Communications Ministries, Colorado Springs, CO 80918
Cook Communications, Paris, Ontario
Kingsway Communications, Eastbourne, England

PATCHWORK FAMILY
© 2001 by Jeanne Zornes for text and Tim O'Toole for illustrations
ISBN: 0-78143-514-5

Edited by Jeannie Harmon
Designed by Granite Design

First printing 2001
Printed in Singapore
04 30 02 01 00   5 4 3 2 1

Patchwork Family

Jeanne Zornes   Illustrated by Tim O'Toole

Equipping Kids for Life

A Faith Parenting Guide is found on page 32.

I heard the *buzz-stop-buzz-stop* as I woke up. "She's sewing again!" I grumbled as I tried to pull my blanket over my head. Would the noise ever stop?

**M**aria sewed and sewed even before she and Papa got married. Sewing was "work" she could do at home while caring for her two children. Veronica and Elias didn't have a dad anymore. So everything Maria sewed paid for rent and food.

T

hen Maria met Papa. Mama had died a long time ago.

"That Maria, she's clever," Papa said when he wore a shirt she'd sewn for his birthday.

Papa and Maria looked so happy at their Valentine's Day wedding. But I was miserable. I itched in the new suit she'd sewn for me. I had to hold this heart-shaped pillow with their rings tied to it. When they put the rings on each others' fingers, my heart felt twisted in two.

I wanted *my* mama back. She'd crawl in bed with me and count stars 'til I went to sleep. Now, I had the top of a bunk bed and no stars to dream on, just cracks in the ceiling.

I burrowed under my covers to find my baby blanket. Mama had made it when I was little. It was faded and ragged. I knew I was too old for it, but it helped me feel better. Holding the blanket made me feel as though Mama was still here next to me.

The first night we slept in the same room, Elias laughed at me. "What a baby! Still has his baby blankie with lambs on it."

I shoved it down by my feet. Elias was five years older. He didn't understand.

I couldn't hear the sewing machine anymore. My sister, Juanita, and Veronica were fussing with their hair in the bathroom. They were just a year apart and good friends now. I wished Elias and I could get along, too.

A yellow-and-brown smell drifted into our room. Maria was fixing cornmeal mush and bacon.

"Miguel! Elias!" she called down the hall. "Breakfast!"

When we came into the kitchen, Maria was stuffing sandwiches into two paper bags. She reached over and hugged me as I walked by. But I didn't hug back. She looked sad as she sat down to eat with us.

The girls and I are going to a fabric sale," she said. "Your dad thought you two could walk over to Beacon Hill to his work site and have lunch with him. Your lunches are ready. He's expecting you."

"Thanks, Mama," Elias mumbled through a mouth full of food. I whirled the brown sugar in my cereal. Maria was always trying to think of things for me to do with Elias. Getting an instant older brother was hard. Being his friend was harder.

"Thanks, Maria," I replied glumly. I couldn't call her *Mama*. Not yet.

Tomorrow is the first Sunday of Lent," she announced, opening the family Bible. "From now until Easter, we need to think about whether or not we live a life that pleases God. He has given us the Bible to help us see who we are inside, and then He helps us change to be more like Him." She started to read from the Bible.

I only half-listened as she read. I knew Maria was doing her best to be a mother to all of us. I knew I wasn't making it easy. I knew that didn't please God. But it was so hard.

**E**lias kept running ten feet ahead of me on the trail over Beacon Hill. He stopped at the top and scowled at me as I collapsed against a tree. My breath came in gasps and I felt dizzy as I looked at the view.

e didn't say anything to each other. As I quit panting, I heard the wind going *whoosh* through the treetops. Heavier branches crackled as they moved from side to side. Below us stretched a green-gray-brown quilt of apartments and homes.

"My dad brought me up here a long time ago." Elias's words stabbed me like a knife. I hadn't thought how much he missed his real father.

"He said to look at the big patchwork picture," Elias added. "Lots of different houses, but one town. And families are lots of different people, but still one family."

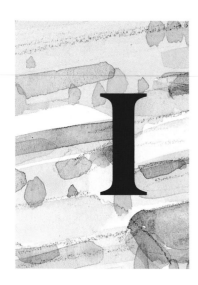

knew he was talking about our family, patched together by Papa and Maria's marriage. I dug my fingers in the dirt. I didn't know what to say.

Elias pulled me up. "The trail's easier going down."

Something else got easier over the next six weeks. I got along better with Elias. Maybe both of us were trying harder.

Easter was close, and Maria was sewing dresses for her customers. Plus, she was sewing dresses for Veronica and Juanita. I went to sleep hearing the sewing machine go *buzz-stop-buzz-stop*. I woke up hearing *buzz-stop-buzz-stop*.

Finally, on the night before Easter, I took my bath, put on my pajamas, and climbed onto the top bunk. Something was different. My old blanket, stained and rough, was gone. In its place lay a new patchwork quilt. I crawled under it, running my hands over its deep softness. The bunk shook, and I turned to see Maria's face near mine. Elias was still in the bathtub, so we were alone.

Do you like it?" she asked. Maria pointed to different squares. "These are scraps from your sisters' new dresses. This was from a shirt your dad said was your favorite. This was your mama's apron. And this," she added, pointing to the lambs, "is the same as your baby blanket. I found the scraps in your mama's sewing boxes."

I touched the square gently. Maria understood. I looked at all the other squares and thought of the patchwork Elias and I saw from the top of Beacon Hill.

"Lots of different people," he'd said, "still one family."

**I** saw the "big picture," the family patchwork. Maria stitched this quilt with a lot of love and a lot of my memories. She was making something new from something old.

I reached under my pillow and pulled out my ragged baby blanket.

"I won't need this anymore," I said. She hugged me, and this time I hugged back.

G ood night, Miguel," she said.

"Good night, Mama."

Faith Parenting Guide

Ages: 4-7

My child's need: To know that God has everything under control even when he or she may not be happy about the circumstances.

Biblical value: Trust

Learning Styles

SIGHT: What special memories did Miguel remember when he saw the new quilt? Do you have a special quilt or blanket that brings special memories to your mind?

SOUND: Repeat the sounds from the sewing machine in the story, *buzz-stop-buzz-stop*. When Miguel heard these sounds, he knew his step-mom was working hard to help others. What sounds do you make when you are helping others (setting the table, raking leaves, watering the flowers, etc.)? What sounds do other family members make (mowing the lawn, washing the car, giving the baby a bath, etc.)? God loves to hear the sounds of people helping others.

TOUCH: Talk about how the mom in this story used the quilt to help Miguel feel good about the family God gave him. Why did holding the blanket help Miguel? Is there something that is special to your family that you can share together? Perhaps making a new photo album, using old pictures and new pictures, will help your family feel more blended together.